CARS
AND
CHRISTIANITY

Stephen Shumate

©Stephen Shumate 2012
All Rights Reserved. No part of this book may be reproduced in any form without permission in writing from the publisher, except in the case of brief quotations embodied in critical articles or reviews.

Unless otherwise noted, Scripture quotations have been taken from THE HOLY BIBLE, NEW INTERNATIONAL VERSION®, NIV® Copyright © 1973, 1978, 1984, 2011 by Biblica, Inc.™ Used by permission. All rights reserved worldwide.

Illustrations by Stacey Heller

ISBN-13: 978-0-9856-9930-7

For more information on Stephen Shumate and his current projects or for booking information for speaking events, send an email to booking@stephenshumate.com or visit www.stephenshumate.com

For More on *Cars and Christianity*
including online discussion and interaction
and other extras, please visit:
www.carsandchristianity.com

South Hampton Publishing
P.O. Box 566
La Vergne, TN 37086

Printed in the United States of America

Cars and Christianity

Contents

Introduction ii

Chapter 1: Restoring Your Beater Car 1

Chapter 2: Your Crew Chief and Spotter 9

Chapter 3: Maintenance 19

Chapter 4: Owner's Manual 25

Chapter 5: New Scratches 29

Chapter 6: GPS 37

Chapter 7: Tow Trucks and Tractor Trailers 43

Chapter 8: Get Going 49

Chapter 9: Exploring on Your Own 56

Introduction

What does it mean to be a Christian? How do you keep from sinning? Isn't God supposed to lead you through life? How do you know what you're supposed to do?

There was a time in my life when I had the mindset that there was no point in trying to be a "good" Christian. I had entirely too many questions and there was way too much to know. I had never liked school and had no intention of spending my free time studying if I didn't have to. My life was busy and I didn't have time to look for answers about Christianity, especially if it was going to tell me I needed to change my lifestyle. I felt I had more important things to do with my free time.

The fact is, life is still pretty busy, and I can't see spending all of my free time studying every book that very smart, Christian men have written. I probably wouldn't understand half of what they were talking about anyhow. I have a job and a family, and what little free time I have is spent with them, working on to-do lists or just catching up on some much needed rest. Besides, it would

Introduction

take a lifetime to study everything that is out there and we were not meant to spend all of our time studying.

However, I would like to understand what it means to be saved, how to have a closer relationship with God and how to be a better Christian and I would like to do these things without having to get a degree in theology. The good news is that I can do these things, and so can you.

You see, Satan is a very clever liar and many of us have fallen for the lie that we don't have the time, the education, or enough interest to have a complete understanding of what it means to be a "good" Christian. So instead, we just ask God into our hearts, live the best we can, and move on with our lives, not giving it a second thought. While it is good for us to be Christians, if we continue to believe this lie and we don't explore our relationship with God, then we will miss out on what it truly means to be a Christian and the joy that comes with it. We will be disgusted with ourselves when we get to Heaven and realize that we did, in fact, have the ability and the resources to understand Christianity.

We don't need a college degree, or even a high school diploma to learn how to be a good Christian and have a great relationship with God. I found this out when I first started thinking about what it meant for me to be a Christian. Furthermore, God showed me that it was actually easier for me to understand Christianity if I tried to think of it in modern day terms instead of in the context of thousands of years ago. This book is the result of how God chose to explain some things to me. I now have a better relationship with God and a better understanding of how

He wants me to live. And I didn't have to take a college course in Christian living either.

One thing you should understand as you read this book is that although this is a book of car analogies, I do not have a deep understanding of how cars work. So please don't ask me how the clutch in the car applies to our spiritual life, because I just don't know. However, please do allow God to connect with you by using examples that resonate in your life. Explore the thoughts and connections that He shares with you. Have a good time, and really enjoy how He reveals what He wants to you to know.

And just an FYI: I do own a 1973 Corvette, I do enjoy working on it, and I do enjoy putting the top down and going for a drive on a nice sunny spring day. So let's get to it and start talking cars and Christianity!

Driver's Check List - *At the end of each chapter, you will find a "Driver's Check List" that will help you accomplish the things that each chapter talks about. The check list is not meant to be a laundry list of things you must do to be a better Christian, but rather it is a suggestion to help you get started in the right direction to your own unique journey of developing a better relationship with God. As with anything, the more effort you put into it, the more you will get out of it.*

Chapter 1: Restoring your Beater Car

The example that I want to start with is an overall picture of what it means to be a Christian, and what happens when we are forgiven. Many of us believe that we are too far gone to ever be able to live like a "good" Christian should. We believe that our lives have gotten so far off track and we have committed so many sins that we will never be able to get our life cleaned up enough to be a "good" Christian; but this is not the case and is just one more lie that Satan feeds us. No matter what you have done in your life, and no matter what your current life looks like, God can and will work with you. You can be the Christian that deep down you want to be.

Let me share my story with you. I became a Christian when I was a child. I don't remember how old I was, but I can remember walking forward and telling one of the adults there that I wanted to be a Christian. I knew I wasn't supposed to sin and if I did I was supposed to ask God for forgiveness. What I didn't realize then, was at that moment I became a new creation (2 Cor. 5:17). When

Cars and Christianity

I became a new creation it was as if God took my old sinful life, threw it away and gave me a new life. Now for the car analogy: It was like I gave my old beat up, used car to God and in return He gave me a brand new car that was in perfect condition. It didn't have a scratch on it.

It then became my responsibility as a Christian to take care of that car by not getting it into accidents and being careful not to get any scratches on it. I was supposed to keep it running well and use it for God. What do I mean by accidents or scratches? I mean sin. You may have heard that sin stains your heart and that God must wash away your sins. In the same way, I am saying that sin scratches and dents your spiritual car and God must be the one to repair it.

For the most part when I was young, I kept my car looking pretty good and I kept it out of trouble. I stayed between the lines on the straight and narrow path. If I did get a bump or a scratch on it I would pray, admit to what I had done and ask for forgiveness. God would then forgive me of that sin. He would buff out the scratch and make it look as good as new (Isaiah 1:18). In other words, I was pretty much a goody two-shoes and didn't get into any trouble. When I was young I was proud of the fact that I tried to live a sin free life. I was proud of the shiny new car that God had given me. I did my best to keep it clean and looking good.

Then there was college. In college, I looked around and there were a lot of cars around me with scratches, dings and dents. And no one seemed to care that their cars were messed up either. Everyone seemed to be having fun and was ignoring the dents and dings. So, at some point in college, I got a scratch on

Restoring your Beater Car

my car but this time I didn't take care of it; after all, everyone else's car had all kinds of scratches, dents and dings. In fact, I didn't necessarily want my car to stick out from everybody else's and look so shiny. I didn't want to be called a goody two-shoes. I wanted my car to look "used" like everyone else's did. I didn't want people to think I couldn't handle having a little scratch or ding on my car. I was in the "Real" world now and this is just how life was in the "Real" world; I wanted to fit in.

So I ended up getting more scratches, dings and dents on my car. What's worse is that I wasn't getting them buffed out either. In fact, I was having fun with my car. I was driving it off-road, no longer between the lines, but rather off of the straight and narrow path. I wasn't too worried about how my car looked. Instead, I was having fun living a life of sin. I didn't worry too much about the sins. After all, they weren't big sins, they were just little scratches. And they weren't any worse than what anyone else had. I had gotten to the point where I cared more about my car blending in with the crowd than I did in taking care of my car the way I should.

Then I graduated from college. Now I was in the "REAL, 'Real'" world and when I looked around at the people I was working and interacting with, most of them had more than just scratches on their cars. They had big dents. So, I thought to myself, "My little scratches are nothing compared to most people," and again, I didn't take care of them. I was having fun driving an off-road course and I was getting brave. After all, God hadn't disowned me. I was still a Christian, right? Life hadn't completely self-destructed because I wasn't living the way God wanted me to. I had a house, a job and enough money to cover my bills plus a little extra to have fun with.

Over time, I became bolder and went further off-course, putting bigger dents in my car. At this point, it was much easier to have fun and wreck my car than it was to try to keep it clean, especially in a world where most people's cars were absolute wrecks. It was much easier to live a life of sin than a life that was pleasing to God. It was much easier to live my life the way most everyone else did, than to live the life I knew I should. I lived that way for many years.

One day I looked in the mirror and I wondered what happened to that kid who cared and used to live an honest life. I looked in the mirror and didn't recognize the car that was looking back. I wondered where the car went that I used to drive and was so proud of.

After some soul searching, I realized that it was still the same car, but I had wrecked it so badly through sin, that I barely recognized it. I realized that my car was smoking, sputtering and barely running at all. I didn't enjoy life, I didn't like what I was doing, but I didn't know how to stop doing those things either. I had been living that way for so long that it was second nature to do things that were harmful to my car. I was no longer proud of my car. In fact, I was ashamed of it. I was ashamed of my life. The reason I was ashamed was because it was a broken down wreck of a car; it was a broken down wreck of a life. I was deeply ashamed of what I had become.

I had two choices. I could continue living the way I was, accepting defeat and believing that's just who I was, or I could turn to God for help. Being a Christian, I knew that God would forgive me of the dents and scratches I had gotten from sinning (I John 1:9). So with my head hung low with shame, I got on my knees (literally) and confessed to God that I was ashamed of who I had become and what I had done. I confessed that I had gotten off His path. I told God that I didn't want to be on the road I was headed down anymore but instead I wanted to get back on His straight and narrow path. I told Him that I was sorry that I had utterly destroyed the brand new car He had given me.

You see, I was broken. But here is the thing... I couldn't fix my car. The fact is the price to get my car fixed was death; a price that we can never pay (Romans 6:23). However Jesus, whose car was perfect and had no scratches, dents, or repairs, is the only one who has the knowledge, the tools, and the ability to fix our cars. He sacrificed His perfect life (car) by dying on the cross, effectively paying the price so that our lives (cars) can be repaired. He died on the cross to fix the dents and scratches that we put on them.

God, being gracious and forgiving, welcomed me back. Even though I was a wreck and my car was barely distinguishable as a car, and certainly not as a Christian car, He welcomed me back with open arms. I was like the prodigal son (Luke 15:11-32). I had followed my own path and had gotten away from God. I did what I wanted to do. I did what I thought was fun, and as a result, I ended up with a car and a life that was absolutely miserable and unsatisfying.

God was happy that I had returned to Him. He graciously fixed my wreck. He certainly didn't have to; it was my choice to go off course. But He fixed it anyway, because He loves me. He forgave me of my sins and He began restoring my car (Psalm 23:3). He forgave me instantly, but He took some time to work out the dents.

Over the next 6 months, He worked out the small scratches, the large scratches, the small dents and the large dents. Some of the dents hurt when He fixed them. Some of the sins He corrected were painful. As He worked out some of the dents that had been there for many years, it brought up memories of some things that I had done a long time ago. He did this for a reason. I had to be sorry for the old sins that I had never taken care of. I had to repent of them in order for Him to forgive me and fix them. So I repented and He fixed every single dent and scratch. He restored me 100% and back into a car that I could once again be proud of. I am pleased to tell you that I am no longer ashamed of my life. God restored my car to original condition. I once again have a car that I can be proud of.

What does your car look like? Have you wrecked it so badly that you hardly recognize it anymore? Are you broken? Maybe your life is not that bad of a wreck, but you have some deep scratches that you need to take care of. Or maybe you have a few small dents from a long time ago.

Regardless of your situation or how damaged you may be, there is good news. Jesus has already paid the price to restore your car to new again. He has already paid the price so that He can erase all of those dents. He will erase them so well that He won't even remember where they were or what they looked like (Psalm 103:12). When He forgives, He forgets; when He fixes your car,

He fixes it so completely that you can't tell where the dents were. No matter how badly damaged your car is, He can and will fix you completely, but you have to go to Him in prayer, admit your brokenness and ask Him to repair you. Then you have to be willing to let Him fix you completely (1 John 1:9).

Driver's Check List: *A new Creation – 2 Corinthians 5:17*
If you are not a Christian and you want to be a new creation (new car)...
Or if you know you need to be restored and are ready to ask God to fix your scratches and dents...

- *Find a quiet place that you can be alone with God.*
- *Get on your knees and bow your head.*
- *Pray (out loud if you can) by having a conversation with God and letting Him know your desires.*
- *Do this right now.*

Cars and Christianity

Chapter 2: Your Crew Chief and Spotter

What's the point of getting our car restored if we are just going to wreck it again? Aren't we are so used to living our life the way we always have that there is no way we can change our bad habits? It's just who we are, right? Well, not exactly.

While the lives we have lived have some impact on our personalities and insights, it does not define who we are and who we are going to be. When you become a Christian, you become a brand new creation (2 Cor. 5:17). You become a brand new car, and while your past experiences will have some effect on your style of driving, it does not have to define the path that you are going to take.

Now that we are a new creation or now that we have been fully restored, we get a new start. We can now start driving like a Christian should, by trying to keep our cars clean and free from scratches. But of course, it's not going to be easy. The world is a dangerous place and everyone around us seems to be continuing on with their accident prone lives. They don't seem to care about our nice new or newly restored car.

So, just how do we avoid messing up our car again? Wouldn't it be nice if there were someone out there who could give us a heads up and help us avoid sin? Well, I am here to tell you that God can help us do just that. He is our crew chief and spotter. Now is the time to open a line of constant communication with God. What do I mean by that? I mean that it's time to pray and then listen. It's time to start training yourself to talk to God and ask for His direction in everything that you do (Proverbs 3:5-6).

It might take some time to get this practice down. You have probably gone for years ignoring God's directions, and instead, you have been doing things you wanted to do based on what you thought was best. I know I did, and that is how I ended up such a wreck. However, once my car was restored and I felt like I was once again living a life that I could be proud of, I wanted to do everything I could to avoid ending up with a car that was broken again. That meant I had to start listening to God so I could avoid sin and that was tough. I wasn't used to taking direction from someone else. I was used to living the way I wanted to, doing what I wanted to do, and not checking in with anyone. I had ignored God for so long that His directions started becoming background noise, and eventually I couldn't hear them at all. When I did try to listen to God, all I could hear was the noise of the world and not His voice. I had to train myself to hear the words and instructions He was giving me.

Before I get into how to hear God's directions, let's first establish the importance of listening to God. If you have ever seen a NASCAR race on TV, it looks like the driver is out there all by himself, driving the car, making his own choices on where to go and how fast to drive. But what you can't see is that the driver is in constant communication with his spotter. Why is that? It's because his spotter can see the entire track, whereas the driver can only see a short distance in front of him. Our life is the same way. We can only see a short way in front of us, but God, who is all knowing (I John 3:20), knows what is about to happen in our life, and knows the best path for us to take.

One of my favorite technologies in racing is the "in-car" camera. If you have ever spent time watching a race, you will know what I am talking about. The "in-car" camera lets you see what the driver sees. And as you spend time watching from this camera's viewpoint you realize that the driver can't see very much of the track. He can only see a short distance in front of him and sometimes he can only barely see that.

So what happens when there is a wreck? The driver, who is going around the track at full speed, comes around a corner and all of a sudden all he can see is smoke and a car sliding across the track sideways. He doesn't know what just happened and he doesn't have a clear view of the track. Now, if the driver relies only on what he can see, what do you think is going to happen? One of two things could happen. The first thing that might happen is that based on what he sees, a big cloud of smoke, he will slow down or come to a complete stop until the smoke and debris is cleared from the track and he knows it is safe to drive forward. The second thing that might happen is that he will make a decision on which part of the track to drive, based only on what he can see. As result of what he can't see because of the smoke, he will likely end up in a wreck.

Neither situation is good. In the first situation, he isn't making any progress, and instead, he ends up sitting on the track with his engine running, not going anywhere. In the second example, he gets into a wreck, which is exactly what we are trying to avoid. Do you know any Christians that go through life this way? When life gets tough, they just shut down and get stuck in a rut; or they charge ahead, making decisions based on what they know, not consulting God or waiting for an answer, and end up getting hurt.

So how do you avoid this yourself? You learn to communicate and listen to your spotter, God. Listening to your spotter is the most important thing you can do, yet many Christians spend all of their time telling God about the problems they see in their life, but they don't listen for His direction. Sometimes they choose to take their own path instead of looking for the path He is trying to get them to take, and sometimes they just shut down.

I did that and what happened to me was when things got tough, I stopped and didn't move at all. I got stuck watching everything happen around me instead of moving forward and making good choices like God was asking me to do. I ended up not making any choices at all. This kept me from getting into a wreck and allowed me to keep my car somewhat free from scratches, so I thought I was being successful at being a Christian. But I was wrong. There is more to being a Christian than just not sinning. I should have listened to God so that I could continue on with His plan for my life instead of just sitting there. I was holding myself back while God was trying to get me to move forward. I wasn't in the race anymore, I was just watching.

You see, the reason I wasn't moving forward in my spiritual life, was because I spent all of my time telling God my problems instead of listening to God so that He could help me through them. I ended up sitting there on the track, telling God what He already knew and didn't give Him any room to tell me how to navigate the track so I could move forward. I would even get upset that God wasn't using me and that I didn't seem to be doing anything with my life.

Imagine what it would look like at a NASCAR race if a driver chose not to listen to his spotter. When he approached a wreck, he would slow down and come to a stop until he could see which way to go. He would be stuck on the track, not going anywhere, while all of the other drivers were speeding past him. He might even end up arguing with his spotter because what he sees in front of him seems to contradict what his spotter is telling him. And instead of trusting that his spotter can see everything on the track and can determine a safe path, he loses faith and trusts his own view more. But, to move forward in the race, the driver must listen to his spotter who has the better vantage point and he must have faith that his spotter will give him clear directions. If he has faith and listens, then he can move forward with confidence, even if he is driving into a little smoke.

We can have this kind of faith and direction in our spiritual life. If we learn how to listen to God as our spotter, He will guide us around those things that will cause sin in our life and He will lead us through dark and smoky situations (Psalms 23). But to be successful in following His directions, we must first listen to His instruction, and then have faith that what He is asking us to do is the best route to follow. We cannot lean on our own understanding (Proverbs 3:5-6) or view of our life. It will be clouded by smoke that Satan puts in our lives. We must rely on God's complete view of our life, even if it means we have to drive through a little smoke.

I want to give you a word of caution from my own experience. Driving through the smoke is scary and dangerous! Think about what goes through the driver's mind as he is in the midst of the smoke. He can't see in front of him, he can't see behind him and he has no idea of what is going on around him, but he does know that if he follows his spotter's directions, he will come out on the other side unharmed and still in the race.

Our Christian life is very much the same way. Satan will cause many distractions all around us. He may cause people close to us to wreck or he may cause someone whose engine is not running well to create a smoke screen in front of us. When Satan puts these distractions around us it can cause us to feel like we do not understand God, because all we see around us is smoke and danger, and yet, He is telling us to move forward. We can't see two feet in any direction and it seems like God is asking us to move in a way that doesn't make sense or into a situation where we can't see and don't know what's going on. But we must have confidence that God doesn't want us to end up in a wreck filled with sin.

Trust me, when we are in the middle of a situation like that, it can be very scary and intimidating. Our natural tendency is to slow down and come to a stop until we feel safe again or to swerve and head in a different direction. And that is just what Satan wants us to do, but we can't let him win. We must move forward. We aren't going to be able to see what's going on around us and we aren't going to be able to see the upcoming debris on the road. But if we truly listen to God, He will guide us through safely because He can see the entire track. He can see the wrecks that we should avoid and He will direct us around them. He is our spotter and He knows that eventually the smoke will clear and that we can make it through safely. And even though it may be scary and may not make sense to us, we can know that His directions are best. He has us in His sights and will lead us through safely (Psalms 23:4).

As I said before, listening to God is one of the most important things we can do. Sometimes, He will tell us to move forward and on what part of the track to drive, but sometimes He will tell us to stop and wait for further instruction (Exodus 14:13). If we don't listen, we will charge head first into the smoke. We will make a judgment call on the lane we should take and before we know it, there will be another car in front of us and we will wreck our car. We might even take a few other people out at the same time. We will end up in a tangled mess of sin, causing other people around us to wreck as well. There have been many churches that have fallen victim to this scenario. It starts with just one or two people, but it ends with many people tangled in the wreckage.

The church usually ends up splitting and losing many members, leaving many of them damaged.

The point is that God, who is our spotter, can see the entire race track. He can and will give us instructions on when to move forward, when to change lanes or when to stop and wait for further instructions so that we may avoid being involved in a sinful, destructive wreck (Luke 11:4). He knows where we need to go and what we need to do in order to be successful. Sometimes His directions will seem contrary to what makes sense to us (Numbers 11:23), but we can know that His directions are much more reliable than what we come up with on our own. His directions are based on the entire track, while our decisions are based on just a small section.

I've been talking a lot about hearing God's directions and there are several chapters in this book that ask you to follow God's path for your life and listen to His voice, so at this point, I want to give you a quick word on how to hear God's instructions. Hearing God's voice is not as easy as listening to our boss giving us directions. Typically God does not speak to us in an audible voice, but He does communicate with us. So how do you know if you are hearing God's instructions? Everyone's experience hearing God will be different, but if you earnestly try to hear God's voice, He will be faithful and teach you how to hear His word. I wrote a blog on this subject once, and my dad left a comment that I really think best sums up what I am trying to say here. His comment was:

"God can use so many methods of communication that we, as individuals, could not know them all; but no doubt He is effective

in getting His message to us. Personally, sometimes I hear that voice through a thought that I know is not my thought. For example, one such thought started with "If I asked you to do something, would you do it?" That was the beginning of a conversation between Him speaking in my thoughts and me replying in my thoughts. I knew it was Him speaking (It would not make sense for me to ask myself that question). I suspect His most used method of communication is thru His word (scriptures read or heard). There are a lot of answers there, but I have experienced that I may have read a verse many times but then when I read or hear it at an appointed time (my terminology), it tells me something I never understood before, giving me direction or guidance. I usually immediately know this is from God."
–Douglas Shumate

The point is that God will find a way to communicate with you. It will take some time for you to become familiar with His voice and learn how He communicates with you, but be patient, because with some practice, you will learn how to understand what He is telling you. We have ignored His voice for so long that it will take time to learn how to distinguish His voice from our own thoughts and all of the useless noise in the world. We will make mistakes while we are learning to hear Him, but if we are patient and faithful enough to keep trying, we will learn to hear His voice and be able to pick it out in a world full of noise. We will be able to distinguish God's truth from Satan's lies.

Imagine all of the noises that a driver hears while in a race, yet he is able to pick out and understand what his spotter is saying to him. It probably took some time for him to learn and distinguish his spotter's voice from the rest of the noises; and no doubt it took some time for him to learn the terminology in order to understand exactly what it is that his spotter is trying to communicate to him, but over time, it becomes second nature. And over time, it can become second nature for us to hear God's instructions as well.

Driver's Check List: *Pray Without Ceasing - 1 Thessalonians 5:17*

- *Be in constant communication with God through your thoughts.*
- *Practice right now, ask Him something through your thoughts.*
- *When you see you are about to be in a situation where you will be tempted to sin, ask God to show you how to avoid or resist it.*

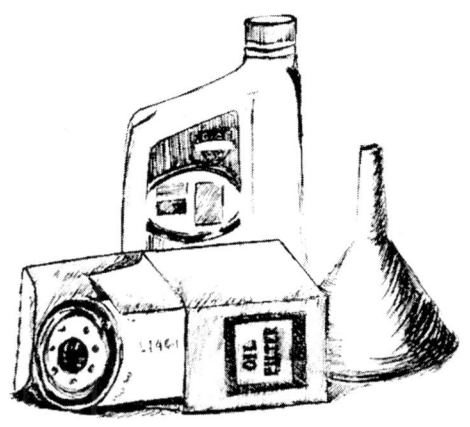

Chapter 3: Maintenance

At this point, our car should be restored, and we should be learning to avoid sin by listening to God. Now we need to get into the mindset of not only avoiding sin, but also maintaining our car. In other words, we want to keep our car running smoothly and at peak performance. If you have gone through the restoration process that we talked about in chapter one, then you know that God has worked out all of the dents and scratches from sin that we had in our life. Now we must turn our attention to our engine. While God is the only one who can repair the damage we have done to our car, it is up to us to maintain it and do our best to keep from damaging it again.

If you were like me, you went for years without giving your spiritual engine any attention. That is to say, you didn't feed your heart with healthy activities or worship. As a result, your interest level in church was low, your interest level in talking about God was low and your interest level in "Christian stuff" was low or even non-existent.

Why is that? It is because you had become like someone who drives an old run-down car. I became this way myself. I was like the guy who continues to drive his car, but does nothing to maintain it. He can't tell you what type of oil he uses, much less the last time he changed it. He is the kind of guy who even gets annoyed when you try to talk about how nice it could be if he would just take a little time to maintain it. He hasn't taken care of his car in a long time and has lost interest in it. I had become the same way with my spiritual life. I hadn't maintained it and as a result I had lost interest in it.

But now that God has restored us, we should begin to become more excited about our spiritual cars. We should be like the people who take meticulous care of their car. They are always excited to talk about it and they keep it maintained with the best oils and fluids available. And once we have this excitement we want to make sure that we don't lose it and let our cars become run-down again.

In order to prevent our excitement from fading, we must take care of our car and give our engines the attention they need. We must maintain our hearts (or our spiritual engines) by routinely doing things that will keep them running at peak performance. We must continually maintain our car for more than just a week, a month, or a year, but we must maintain it for the rest of our lives. I know too many people who think that as long as they ask God into their heart, and don't do anything too stupid, then they have done all that they need to do. But that is like restoring a car

Maintenance

and then never doing any maintenance on it. It will eventually end up much like it was before the restoration.

What happens if you never change the oil in your car or do anything to maintain the engine? It will eventually cause a breakdown. The oil will slowly deteriorate and if it is not changed it will lead to engine failure. Before too long, you will find yourself on the side of the road, going one mile per hour with smoke pouring from your tailpipe and when you try to step on the gas, you won't know if it is going to lurch forward or stop altogether.

So what happens when you don't go to church and worship or do those things that have a positive effect on your heart? Eventually, your joy and excitement will break down, and your spirit will be broken. Your engine will begin to run rough, and you will begin to struggle to keep interested in the things that you are supposed to be doing. Eventually, that will lead to sin, the very thing we are trying to avoid. Before too long, you will find yourself on the side of the road of life, with your world crashing in on you. Your life will be going one mile an hour with anger, hatred or frustration pouring from your heart.

Have you ever felt like that? Was that your life before your restoration? Chances are you were feeling that way before God restored your car, because you hadn't been maintaining your spiritual engine. When God restored your car, He got your spiritual engine in good running order as well. Suddenly, your spirit felt good, and you experienced the joy of the Lord. And now you are on fire for God and you feel like you could run the race forever. But if we don't take time to maintain our engine, we will end up burned out. We will end up back on the side of the road again, not going anywhere, wondering where our fire went or why our spirit seems so broken.

We must also avoid maintaining our engine with the wrong things. If we feed our spirit unhealthy fluids, then it will have a negative result. It would be like putting diesel fuel in a gasoline engine; it will cause the engine to shut down. Similarly, if we are a Christian but we constantly listen to music or watch movies that promote sex, drugs, and hate then it will break down our spiritual engine. If we continue to take part in crude jokes or lusting for the opposite sex, it will cause spiritual problems. If we continue going to bars and drinking excessively, then we will lose our enthusiasm for spiritual things. So we must not only maintain our engine, we must also avoid harmful additives as well. We must stop filling our lives with unhealthy, negative, and sinful influences, and replace them with positive, Christ centered activity and worship.

The good news is that there are things that we can do on a regular basis that will help keep our car running smoothly, so that we don't have to constantly go to God with "major" issues when we could have avoided them in the first place. So, what are the things you need to do to maintain your engine? There are some basics things that you should know about, and then there are some things that are specific to your engine. Some of the basic activities that we all should do, as Christians, are things like: going to church and worshipping, helping others, giving back to God, and doing devotions. These are all things that exercise our emotions and heart. We cannot forget that they are as much a part of our car as the doors, wheels and windshields.

Maintenance

By the same token, we must be careful that we don't fall into the trap of just going through the motions. When we just go through the motions, it is as if we pop the hood and look at the engine but never actually do any maintenance, which accomplishes nothing. If we go to church and don't actively worship or listen, but instead we just show up and allow our minds to wander and think about what is going on at work or what we are going to have for lunch, then we are not maintaining our engines. Instead we are just going through the motions of what a Christian is supposed to do, without actually doing them.

There are many other things that we can do to keep our engines running smoothly, but each of our engines is different and requires different care. For instance, my spiritual engine runs better when I listen to worship music and take time to enjoy the songs, however, I know other people who benefit from reading spiritual blogs and doing Bible studies. God, who created our engines and knows them inside and out, can help us understand what our specific engine needs are. After all, He is not only our Crew Chief and Spotter; He is also our Chief Mechanic. So be sure to pray and ask Him to show you what you need to do to keep your engine running smoothly.

Driver's Check List: *Treasure Your Car - Matthew 6:21*

- ☐ *Find a church to visit and start going every week.*
- ☐ *Do your best to actively participate in worship at church.*
- ☐ *Once you find a church that you feel is right for you, get engaged and volunteer to help in some way.*
- ☐ *Be sure to make new friends there. You can help keep each other accountable.*
- ☐ *Pray and ask God to show you what else you can do to help your engine continue to run smooth.*

Cars and Christianity

Chapter 4: Owner's Manual

There is a ton of things to know about your new life/car, and there is no possible way to cover everything you need to know in this short book. So, what do you do, how do you learn about your new life/car? Wouldn't it be helpful if life came with a manual? Well, you are in luck, it does. The Bible is God's word, and we are His creation just like a manual is the manufacturer's word, and the car is the manufacturer's creation. So from this example, we can say that the Bible is to us, what a manual is to a car. It gives us definitive, concrete information on what our car is capable of, how to use it, and what we can do to maintain it. The Bible is the MOST important book for our lives. It is the manual for our Christian life.

Almost everything comes with a manual these days, and almost no one ever reads them. So what is the point of having a manual in the first place? A manual not only gives us directions on how to use a product, but it also tells us how to take care of it. It gives us warnings and sometimes it will even tell us about a feature we never knew it had.

To give you an example, let's say that you bought a tool, such as a voltmeter. For years, you used it to measure voltage. If you needed to make sure an outlet or lamp was working, you went to your workbench and grabbed your trusty voltmeter and used it to make sure that you were getting the correct voltage. But then one day, you run across your manual, and you start reading it. All of a sudden, you realize that your voltmeter will do much more than just measure voltage. It will measure continuity and resistance, check diodes, and do things you don't have a clue as to how to do. But if you should ever come across the opportunity to measure your phase angle, you now know that you have the tool to do the job.

Well, guess what; the Bible can do the very same thing for us. There are things that you may not realize that you are capable of as a Christian, but if you read your Bible, you will begin to learn how to do those things. You may have never realized that you are equipped to witness to people (Matthew 5:13-16), but as you read the Bible, you will gain the knowledge on how to witness. You may not realize that you are equipped to comfort people (2 Corinthians 1:3-7), but if you read the Bible, you will learn how to explain the comfort of God to others. There are many things that you are capable of but may not realize, and the Bible can help you reach your full potential (Mark 11:22-25).

Our manual also gives us warnings. While it may be common sense not to use your voltmeter underwater, it may not be as clear that it could cause physical harm if you tried an "in-circuit current measurement where the potential to earth is greater than 1000V" (according to the Fluke 87 True RMS Multimeter User Manual). And while it may be clear to us as Christians that we shouldn't be involved in some activities that are sinful or that lead to sin, it may not be clear that we need to be careful of false teachers (Romans 16:17-18), or that we shouldn't boast about what we do (James 4:13-17). There are many other warnings in the Bible as well, and it is important for us to be aware of them.

The Bible is the most comprehensive book available for us today and it is more versatile than anything else out there. It can also be used for diagnostics. Despite our best efforts to maintain our engines there will still be times when we start to run rough. When this happens we turn to our manual (The Bible) and look for answers on what may be causing problems for our spiritual engines. Our manual will help us with diagnostics and give us direction on how to correct the problem.

As I said earlier, most people don't read their manuals and a lot of Christians don't read their Bible either. Many Christians today wait until their car or their spirit is running so rough that it is on the verge of breaking down before they turn to the Bible for answers. Instead, what they should be doing is constantly reading their Bible. If they did, they would be aware of warnings that might have helped avoid the problem in the first place. Or they would immediately know what to do or where to find the answer if something does come up unexpectedly in their life. Imagine how much time we would waste looking for an answer in a car manual if it were as large as the Bible and we didn't know where to find the answer. Or what would happen in a race if the

Cars and Christianity

pit crew had to look up how to change a tire during a race? It would be very time consuming and wasteful, not to mention the anxiety it would cause the driver while waiting for an answer. We can avoid a lot of heartache and worry by knowing what is in our Bible and where to find it.

We certainly will not understand everything in the Bible the first, second or even third time we read through it, but we must stick with it. It will take some time to get used to the language and instruction, just like it would take us some time to learn how to understand a car manual if we had never read one before. But God will help us understand the things we need to know at the time we need to know them. And if you continue to read and study, you will be preparing yourself for things you never knew you could do and you will be ready to do whatever it takes to keep your car in the race.

If God gave us a manual, then we should do our best to read and understand it. There are many reading plans and websites that can help you pick a plan and a timeframe that will work for you. Since it is our manual for life, it is the most important book we can read. If you have never read the Bible all the way through, I beg you to start immediately. Even if you don't understand everything that you read, go to the effort of reading it from cover to cover.

Driver's Check List: *All Scripture is Useful - 2 Timothy 3:16*

- *Find a Bible. You can find one online at www.biblegateway.com or www.youversion.com.*
- *Find a reading plan (you can find one online at the above websites).*
- *Set a goal to complete your reading plan.*
- *Start reading just as soon as you can, start today if possible...even if you don't fully understand what you are reading, do it anyway.*

Chapter 5: New Scratches

Even though we are Christians, and we are trying our best to live the life that God wants us to, it is not always going to be easy and we are not always going to be able to avoid tough situations. No matter how hard we try, we will end up with a new dent or scratch from sin in our lives. We are, after all, only human. Fortunately, when this happens, it is not the end of the world, but it does mean that we have a little work to do.

When this happens, it is important for us to ask God to take care of that dent or scratch right away. We do this by understanding what we did wrong, having the desire not to do it again, and then admitting our sin to God (this is the process known as repenting: feeling and expressing sincere regret or remorse about your sin). We must then ask for His forgiveness, and allow Him to repair us.

But why is it important if it is just a small scratch? No one will really notice, will they? Why does it matter? Your life is nobody else's business but yours and God's, and besides, He loves us regardless, right? These questions are full of misconceptions and Satan loves to use them to deceive us.

The first misconception is that God loves us regardless of how badly we screw up, so it doesn't matter if we have a little sin in our lives. While it is true that God fully loves us despite how we mess up, if we think having unforgiven sin doesn't matter then we are mistaken. God sent His son, Jesus, to earth in order to pay for our sin (John 3:16). Jesus paid for our sin by living a perfect life here on earth, then sacrificing Himself in our place. He was beaten and whipped, then hung on a cross until He died, so that He can fix every scratch and dent that we put on our car, even the little ones. If God went through this much effort and suffering for us, so that He could fix all of our scratches and dents, then it must be important for us to go to Him to be repaired.

God does love us despite the sin we have in our life. He took the time to restore our car. He got us back on the right track and made us as good as new. He did this because He loves us. But if we stop with just this statement we are leaving out the rest of the truth. You see, He loves us like a parent loves their child. But just like a parent can be hurt and disappointed by their child's actions, God can also be disappointed and hurt by our actions.

Even though we may disappoint Him sometimes by sinning, He still loves us. Let me give you an example. Imagine a boy who has been playing in the mud for a long time. He is covered from head to toe in mud, and one day he comes home with his clothes stained brown. His parents clean him up and give him new clothes. He really likes his new clothes and the way they feel. His parents warn him not to go near the mud anymore because he will ultimately end up with mud on his nice new clothes. At first, he listens to their warnings and does a great job avoiding the mud. But one day, he gets bold and ignores his parents' warning; he gets too close to the mud puddle and ends up with a large mud stain on his shirt.

He goes back home, disappointed that he ruined his new shirt. When he gets there, his parents ask what happened. He admits that he got too close to the mud and ruined his shirt. He tells them how sorry he is and asks them to clean his shirt again. Of course we all know the parents' reaction. They are disappointed that he didn't follow their warnings and then they might discipline him, but ultimately they will replace his shirt with a new one.

Does their disappointment mean they don't love him anymore? Absolutely not. Does the fact they discipline him mean they love him any less? On the contrary, it means that they love him enough to try to correct his behavior. If the child doesn't allow his parents to take care of the mud stain, will they see it every time they see him? You bet, and it will be a constant reminder to them of how he didn't listen to their warnings and instead, disobeyed them.

This is our story if we don't go to God, admit what we did, accept his discipline, and then allow Him to fix the scratch. Surely He will be disappointed, but does that mean He loves us any less? Absolutely not. He may discipline us, but does this mean He hates us? On the contrary, the Bible says we should be worried if He doesn't discipline us (Revelation 3:19). If we allow this sin to remain in our life, He will see it every time He looks at us. Since God is perfect and holy, having this stain of sin, no matter how small, will cause separation between us and Him. And the further away from God we are, the closer we are to the sinful life He rescued us from. So don't fall for the partial truth that because God loves us no matter what we do, we don't have to worry about the little sins. He does love us no matter what we do, but we do need to take care of ALL of our sins.

The second misconception is that it is not a big deal to us if we don't take care of sin. We think that because we "know" what we did wrong, we don't need to repent and ask for forgiveness. The problem with this line of thinking is that it is a slippery slope. We start with one little scratch and then we add another little scratch. Well, now we have two scratches, so what's the harm in one more? The next time, it's a little dent, and before we know it, we are back where we started in chapter one. Not taking care of sin is a slippery slope, and if we are not careful, we will end up a complete wreck again. I cannot begin to express how dangerous it is to have this mind set. Since we covered this in the first chapter, I won't spend any more time discussing it here, but if you have any doubt in your mind, please re-read chapter one.

The final problem that I want to cover is when we think our life is no one else's business. It is true that the Bible tells us we need to pay more attention to the sin in our own life than the sin in someone else's life (Matthew 7:5). At the end of the day, our heart and our sin is a matter that will be settled individually between us and God (I Samuel 16:7). But until that day, what we do and how we act, as Christians, is being watched by the rest of the world (John 15:19).

While it would be nice for the rest of the world to follow the Bible's teaching and pay more attention to what is going on in their own life than what is going on in ours, that's just not how the world works. Once we have made a public decision that we are Christians, we put ourselves out there, where the rest of the world can judge us, like it or not. But we shouldn't hide that we are Christians either. Being out in the world is where we are supposed to be because we are instructed in the Bible to be witnesses to others. And we cannot be a witness to others if we are hiding who we are.

But imagine how effective our witness is if we have scratches and dents on our car; a car that is supposed to be clean. Do you think they will want to take the same path that we have taken? Dave Ramsey puts it this way, "You wouldn't take financial advice from a broke person, and you wouldn't take dieting advice from an overweight person." And I would add that you wouldn't take spiritual advice from someone who has a bunch of unresolved sin in their life.

Would you take advice on how to get your car cleaned up from someone who has lots of dents and scratches all over their car? Will someone else take your advice on getting their life back in order if you have unresolved issues in your life?

Imagine what we look like to the rest of the world. We went for a long time driving a beat up, wreck of a car, but then we got our car fixed, cleaned up, and running well. That should inspire others to do the same. But will it inspire them if we just end up back where we started, or will it cause them to wonder what the point is if, in the end, nothing is going to change. There is a good chance that it will actually turn some people off of going through a restoration like we did, if they believe that in the end their car is going to end up a dirty wreck again. They might think that you went through a lot of work and had to follow a lot of rules just to end up back where you started.

If we don't take care of the sin in our life, even the sin we think no one knows about, we run the risk of turning people away from God. We won't carry the appearance that we are Christians, and after a while, people may even forget that we are Christians, because our cars don't look any different than theirs. Don't get me wrong, I'm not saying we need to make sure everyone knows how "good" we are, but what I am saying is that if people know we are Christians and our cars appear trashy, then there is a good chance they are going to call us hypocrites and wonder why we don't live like Christians should. They are not going to want to go through what we did and they are not going to want to become a Christian. What we do may not technically be any of their business, but it does affect how they view God and Christianity. And that might just be enough to prevent them from starting a relationship with God.

So as you can see, if we believe that we can have a little sin in our lives, or that we don't need to go to God and ask for forgiveness for all sins, no matter how small they may seem, or that what we do has no impact on anyone else, we are mistaken. It is very important that we take care of any and all sin in our life as soon as we can, by repenting and asking for forgiveness. We do this so we can keep a close relationship with God instead of ending up on a slippery slope back to sin and that way we can be an effective witness for God.

Driver's Check List: *Taking care of our Sins - Luke 3:4*

- *Go to God in prayer today and ask Him to forgive any outstanding sin in your life.*
- *Practice and develop the habit of asking for forgiveness as soon as you realize and are sorry for your sin.*

Cars and Christianity

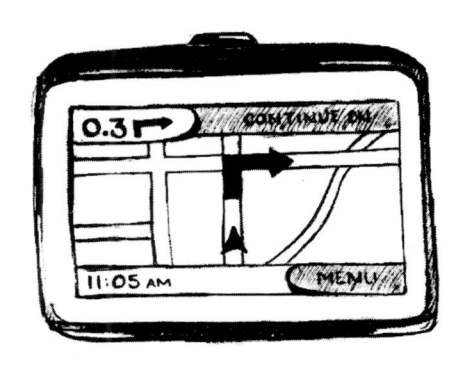

Chapter 6: GPS

Okay, so our car has been restored, we have learned how to avoid potholes and roadblocks, and we are maintaining our engine. Where do we go from here? We have already talked about listening to God as our spotter in order to avoid sin in the short term, but now we want to talk about the long term direction in our life.

You may be wondering what the major difference is between "Listening to Your Spotter" and "Using your GPS." Let me tackle that first, because they are similar. Listening to our spotter is a day to day thing. It is about avoiding the potholes and debris that is in the road immediately in front of us that will cause us to sin. However, following our GPS is actively listening to God to know which roads to take. It is about deciding what direction we should take with our life and what long term decisions we should make.

We need our GPS because our Christian life shouldn't just keep us going around in circles like a NASCAR race. There is a point to our life, and God has put together a plan for each of us (Ephesians 2:10). In fact, He already has a plan ready for you. It is now up to you to decide if you want to follow His plan or if you want to continue following your own plan for life.

Satan loves for us to believe the lies that life doesn't have a specific direction and that YOU have to figure out what to do with your life all by yourself, but this is simply not true. God already has a plan laid out for you, and if you follow His plan and lean on Him for direction then He will make sure your needs are taken care of (Philippians 4:19). Sometimes this is easier said than done!

So how do we hear and follow God's direction? We refer to our GPS. What is our GPS? Well, I like to refer to my GPS as my "God Positioning System." I want to live my life and serve God in the way that He wants me to. In order to live my life this way, I must be where He wants me to be, doing what He wants me to do. That sounds very easy to do, but it takes time to learn how to hear and understand God's direction for our lives.

I want you to think back to the first time you used a GPS. If you were like me, it took you a little while to get used to using it and to understand exactly where and when it wanted you to turn. You might think that this would be easy since it gives us turn by turn directions, but I am willing to bet that you have, at least on one occasion, missed a turn that your GPS was trying to get you to take. We have all heard that little voice say, "Recalculating Route."

Well, guess what, our God Positioning System works the same way. It takes a little time to get used to hearing God's voice, especially since it isn't a physical voice. But over time, just like we learned how to follow the GPS in our car, we can learn to follow God's instructions for us. And if we miss a turn and get off His path, He will give us a new set of directions to get us back on His plan.

How does this system work? Well, let's start from the beginning. When we turn on our GPS, the first thing we do is tell it where we want to go. It then figures out where we are and once it has located our starting position, it figures out the best path to our destination. Then it gives us directions and when we come to an intersection, it tells us which way to go. Sometimes it tells us to take a turn off of a perfectly good road that seems to be headed in the right direction. Why does it do that? It does that because it knows that if we stay on the path we are on, while it may seem to be headed in the right direction, ultimately will take us off course and somewhere we don't want to be.

Our life is much the same way. God knows where we are. We took care of that when our car was restored. Now we have to tell God that we choose His plan as our destination instead of the plan that the world would have us choose. This is an important step that we cannot skip. God loves communication and while He knows our hearts, He wants us to confess with our mouth our desire (Romans 10:9). That is to say we need to verbally commit to God that we want His plan for our life and that we are committed to stay on that plan to the best of our ability. This is an admission that we need Him and that we cannot do it on our own. When we do this, we are allowing Him to enter the destination that He has chosen for us into our "GPS".

Our "GPS" will not work with any destination other than the one God has for us. If we choose a different destination and seek out things like power, wealth or fame then we are choosing to follow a worldly path. And these paths can take on many forms. They aren't just power, wealth and fame but they can also be security, success at any level or anything that takes our focus off God, even our own family. Satan will make these paths look very appealing or even necessary and he can even make them look like they are headed in the right direction. So we must be careful that we are listening to God when we choose to follow a path. And while the path God has for us may include wealth, power or success, these things are neither our goal nor the focus of our desired destination. God's path leads to a spiritual goal, not a worldly one. That means that instead of our goal being focused on chasing our own desires, it is focused on following God's plan for our lives.

If we choose a worldly path as our goal and focus, God will not lead us down that path. Instead, we will be following our own wants and desires which can be influenced by Satan. Remember, God is all knowing and all powerful (Psalm 147:4-5, Matthew 19:26) and He knows where all paths lead. He is the beginning and the end. We, on the other hand, can only guess where a path might lead. Satan knows this and is the king of misdirection. He will exploit our tendency to rely on our own understanding and he will make the other paths look good to us, in the hopes that we will follow our best guess instead of asking God for directions. That is why it is so important for us to rely on God and His knowledge rather than to rely on our own understanding which is limited and can be influenced by Satan.

Once we have accepted God's destination and entered it into our "God Positioning System" by confessing to God, through prayer, our desire for His path for our life, what do we do next?

We listen to God for direction. Now, as I said earlier, it will take some time to learn how to hear God's voice. God speaks to us in different ways. Sometimes it will be in an overwhelming feeling as in: I really have this feeling that God wants me to go to a specific church, or I have an overwhelming feeling that taking this job is right. Sometimes He will speak to us through His word, and as we are reading the Bible, a direction will become clear to us and He will allow us to understand what He wants. Sometimes, God will even use other people to help spark the ideas and thoughts He wants us to have. Over time, you will begin to recognize when God is trying to tell you something. Keep in mind that He may not give us immediate direction; He may take some time to reveal His path to us. So we must remain patient and wait for His instruction.

Here is the key thing to remember: when He speaks to us and gives us direction, we must follow it. If we don't, we might end up back where we started or somewhere we don't want to be. From time to time we will get off course, and when we do, we need to make sure we tune back into what God is telling us. He will recalculate the route and get us back on His path, but only if we seek His direction. He is not going to force us to stay on track. He will help us if we are earnestly trying to follow His directions.

But if we do not put forth an effort to hear and follow His path, He will not force us to.

We need go to God in prayer to ask for His guidance. We need to continually check with our "God Positioning System" to see what direction He wants us to take. And we need to be sure that we follow His directions. If we are tuned into His voice, He will give us direction and we can know that we are on the path to living His plan for our life. We should constantly be checking that we are on the path that God wants us to be on.

Driver's Check List: *Getting on God's Plan - Ephesians 2:10*

- ☐ *If you are ready to commit to living God's plan for your life, instead of your own, Pray right now and tell God.*
- ☐ *Learn to hear God's directions by praying and meditating on major decisions in your life.*
- ☐ *Follow His directions and have faith that they are right for you.*

Chapter 7: Tow Trucks and Tractor Trailers

Through the years I've had friends who drive big rigs, tow trucks, sports cars, and mini vans. Each person is as different as the car they drive. Each person has different strengths and weaknesses, personalities and interests. And just as there are many different types of cars on the road today there are many different types of Christians. That's right; not every Christian has the same abilities and strengths. Instead, we are designed for different purposes (Romans 12:4-8).

You see, every vehicle is designed for a specific task. A tow truck is designed to help cars that get stuck get back on the road again. Tractor trailers are designed to carry important, heavy loads. Sports cars are designed to go fast and win races, while minivans are designed to help transport large groups from one place to another.

Cars and Christianity

When we were created, we were created with specific strengths and abilities (Romans 12:6). God has created us with a specific purpose in mind (Ephesians 2:10). You may be designed as a spiritual tow truck and have the natural talent and ability to help people when they get stuck in their Christian life or you may be designed as a tractor trailer and be used to support the church in a heavy lifting sort of way. You may be a sports car and be designed to run short hard races by working really hard for God in short spurts, then resting and rebuilding for your next race or you may be a minivan and have the natural talent to help children get started on the right road. No matter what our natural ability may be, God has a purpose for our life.

There are many Christians who never realize this concept. You see, Satan has put into the world the misconception that being a Christian is all about being a "good" person. Some people even go so far as to say that Christianity is just about not doing "bad" things and that we don't have to do "good" things or serve God, instead we just have to stay out of trouble. He has put the thought out there that God doesn't want us to have to work hard and get dirty, and that God doesn't care if we are lazy or hardworking Christians. These are lies; nowhere in the Bible does it say that once we become a Christian life gets easy. The Bible talks about earning crowns and treasures in heaven (2 Timothy 4:7-8). It talks about taking care of the needy, the hungry, the poor and the widowed (Matthew 25:34-46). It tells us we need to spread the word of God (Matthew 28:19-20) and teach our children the ways of the Lord (Proverbs 22:6). It talks about being vigilant and being ready for His return (Matthew 22:42-44). It doesn't say that once we become Christians that we are done and have fulfilled our purpose, instead it says it is just the beginning.

Many people quote the verse that says all we need is faith to be saved (Ephesians 2:8-9) in order to justify their inaction. And while it is true that we have to have faith in God to be saved, we must not forget the verse that says faith without works is dead (James 2:26). You see, God is going to ask us to put our vehicle to work. And if our faith is NOT dead, then not only will we be willing to serve God, we will actually have a desire to work for Him.

If you restored a race car and got it running the best you could, would you want to keep it in a garage where only you could see it? Or would you want to take it for a ride, put it in a race and actually let the car run like it should? I know that if I put the time and effort into rebuilding a car, I would want to drive it as often as possible. If I took the time to install air conditioning, I would want to turn it on when it's hot and if I took the time to install a hitch on the back of my car, I would want to tow things. If we don't put those things to good use then our work is for nothing, and our effort is "dead."

If your faith is working properly, you will want to get out there and do what you were created to do; you will want to put your car to good use. Don't worry if you don't feel this way yet. God may still be growing or re-building your faith. You may still be in the process of being restored, but soon, you should start experiencing this desire. Regardless of whether you are in the rebuilding stages or if your faith is having a hard time getting started, if you want your faith to be alive instead of dead, then pray and ask God to restore your faith. Remember what God tells us, "Ask and it will be given to you" (Luke 11:9-10).

So how do you figure out what kind of car you are? Well, that is the tough part. Sometimes it is glaringly obvious what your strengths are and sometimes it is not. Sometimes what you are naturally good at in the secular world is not what you are designed for in the Christian life. The only way to really know what purpose your car has is by seeking God's direction.

The Bible says, "Seek and you will find" (Matthew 7:7). If you seek out how you can serve God and the purpose He has for your life, He will show you. This is really the key to all of the chapters in this book. You see, the key to understanding Christianity is in seeking that understanding. God wants to show you the plan He has for you. He didn't create your plan, your job, YOUR ministry, just to keep you in the dark, but you have to want it, and you have to seek it. God is not going to force it on you.

It may take a while for you to realize what your ministry is, and your ministry may change directions as you go through life, but if you continue seeking, you will be able to serve God in a mighty way. God took three to four years to restore and train me, and it was only after those years that I began to realize how He intended for me to use my car. Now I feel I am doing what He created me to do. And if at some point His plan takes me in a different direction, I will be happy to re-train and do that job too.

So be patient and do your best to learn the things that God is trying to teach you. If we practice the things He teaches us, and we keep our faith in good running order, then one day we will realize that we are no longer practicing and preparing to run the race, but instead we will find that we are fully engaged in the purpose and plan God has for us. I can tell you from experience that once you are fully engaged in this way, you will feel alive, enthused and excited about your life and where it is headed because you will be fulfilling the purpose you were created for.

Drivers Check List: *Finding Our Abilities - Romans 12:6*

- *Be patient and attentive to what God is asking you to do.*
- *Look for the opportunities that God puts in your life, so that you can practice and prepare for your specific task.*

Cars and Christianity

Chapter 8: Get Going

This chapter is perhaps one of my favorites. It really brings together a concept that I think many people overlook, even though it is one of the most important to understand. It is summed up by the greatest commandment in the Bible "...Love the Lord your God with all your heart and with all your soul and with all your mind." (Matthew 22:37).

This means we need to love God with our heart through our faith and worship, we need to love God with our mind through church and study of the Bible, and we need to love God with our soul by putting what we believe into action. When I started thinking about my Christian life and my relationship with God in this way, it really clarified for me the areas that I really needed to work on. Let's look at this in a car example and see if it does the same for you.

Loving God with our mind is like going through driver's education. We had to study and be able to pass a written test to show we had a working knowledge of driving before we could get behind the wheel of a car. The idea is that if we don't have any knowledge about how to drive, or about the car itself and the dangers of being on the road, then we won't be successful at driving. We must have a working knowledge of the car and how to drive, not just have a desire to drive. Loving God with our mind is the same way. We need to study the Bible and have a working knowledge of God and Christianity, and not be satisfied with just having a desire to be saved.

Paul says that we should learn these things so that we can be prepared to give a defense (I Peter 3:15), which simply means if someone asks us why we are a Christian or why we act the way we do, then we can give an answer. Of course we cannot be expected to know everything there is to know. Even a race car driver doesn't know what every single bolt on the car is for and we cannot be expected to understand everything that God does and how He works. But we can strive to learn and know that God will give us what we need to know when we need to know it (Luke 21:14-15).

Loving God with our hearts is loving God with our emotions. When you don't love God with your emotions you won't have faith in Him and you will constantly be looking for alternatives. One group of people who fall in this category will often call themselves spiritual but not religious. They may believe that there is a god, but they don't go to church. They tend to place more emphasis on themselves and self-discovery than in faith in a god. But not having faith in God is like a driver who has no confidence that his car will make it to the finish line. Instead, he looks for others ways to get there. He might try a bicycle or even walking, but the truth is that unless he is in the car God has given him, there is no chance that he will finish the race. He will end up being left on the track, working harder than ever and succeeding in nothing. I call this overachieving at underachieving. We must love God with our hearts so that we can have faith in Him and His word in order to finish the race.

Loving God with our soul is where the rubber meets the road. It is actually getting in the car and driving. It is actually putting the car in drive and stepping on the gas and doing it. It is not just talking about God, but it is actually serving Him. It is about volunteering at church, it is about cleaning up your life and working hard at avoiding sin (Satan doesn't make this easy on us). It is about picking up your Bible and starting to read it. It is about doing whatever God is laying on your heart to do, and doing it with your best effort. A driver who knows how to drive but never gets in the car to go anywhere is not in the race. Instead, he is just watching all of the other drivers go by.

If we try to leave out any of these parts, it will end in failure. If I don't know how to drive, when I get in the car and step on the gas, I will wreck. If I don't have faith in my car, I will be looking for alternatives. And if I don't get in the car and actually drive, then I will end up just sitting there. In all of these scenarios we come up short of the finish line.

Most Christians love God with their heart enough to have some faith in Him. Some Christians love God with their mind enough to know why they should serve Him, but there are fewer Christians who love God with their Soul enough to get out there and do something about it. Some even get intimidated into non-action. They worry about what their friends will think of them if they become one of "those" Christians. So they don't take the time to love God through study like they should. And when it comes time to step out on faith and love God with their heart, they sit there quietly making excuses for their inaction. And instead of giving up their "free" time to serve God in a public way, they just write a check on Sunday and call it a day.

For many years I didn't bother loving God with my mind. I knew just enough to know that He died on the cross for my sins, but I didn't take the time to really understand why that was important. I didn't take the time to learn the dangers of the slippery slope of sin. And I didn't love God with my heart enough to care that I had a life full of sin and was sliding even further away from Him. And when God did bring me to my knees, I almost didn't love Him with my soul and I nearly allowed Satan to intimidate me into non-action.

God showed me that I had a wreck of a life and that it was time for change. It was essentially a Holy Intervention. And when it came time for me to make a decision to choose my way or His way, I remember thinking "Am I really going to do this? Am I really going to change my life and be a 'Real' Christian? What will my friends think?"

I had the same feeling in the pit of my stomach that people who go bungee jumping for the first time get when they step to the edge of the platform and look down. In front of me was an exciting relationship with God that I had never had before, and behind me was the sinful life I had gotten so used to. The fear we feel when it comes time to make this decision is from Satan. He desperately does not want us to choose God's path. He wants us to remain inactive Christians. So he exploits our fear of change. He makes the mess of a life that we are living seem better than the life God offers us. He uses our fear of change and failure to hold us captive to our old sinful or inactive life.

He did this to the Israelites as they were fleeing captivity. They had been slaves to the Egyptians being forced to work in harsh conditions, being whipped and punished for not finishing impossible tasks. But after they had escaped and as they were fleeing in the desert, they began thinking to themselves "...It would have been better for us to serve the Egyptians than to die in the desert!" (Exodus 14:12). They started thinking that it would be better to be overworked slaves than to be in the desert headed towards the promise land. Satan clouded their minds with smoke and mirrors and showed them death, even though God had promised them a land flowing with milk and honey (Exodus 3:17).

Satan will try to do the same things to us. He will cloud our vision with being picked on, poverty, failure, and a life without any fun, but God has promised us so much more. Satan will try to convince us that staying on the platform and not taking the leap of faith is better and safer for us than to commit to serving God. He will tell us that the comfort of the familiarity of our sinful life is much better than the unknown of where God will take us. The question becomes, do you trust in what your spotter, who is God, is telling you, or in the deception that Satan is showing you? Is it better to stay in the sinful, destructive, or inactive life you are living or to endure change by trusting in God and taking a leap of faith?

When I decided to trust in God and took the leap of faith by saying yes to cleaning up my life and following God, I got the same exhilarating thrill that people get when they bungee jump. It has been and continues to be the most exciting and joyful thing I have ever done. It was hard to make the decision, but in the end, it is clearly the right decision.

We cannot let Satan intimidate us into non-action. If we do, we run the risk of knowing how to drive, believing that we can drive, but never actually getting in the car and doing the things that God wants us to do. As a result, we will end up accomplishing nothing. We will become couch potato Christians. The Bible calls this being "Luke Warm" and warns us against becoming this way (Revelation 3:16). When we become a couch potato Christian, Satan wins a battle because when we are inactive, we are not serving God. If we are not serving God then we are not spreading His word to bring more people into the kingdom of God. Instead, Satan will continue to keep them in his control. Sometimes we think that our in-action doesn't harm anyone but ourselves, but what we are doing by sitting idly by is watching our friends, family, and neighbors head straight for destruction. Our in-action can lead to their spiritual death. I'm not saying that we have the power to save people, only Jesus can do that, but we can point them in the direction of His saving grace. We can show them another way.

As we discovered earlier, our cars have a purpose; so it is up to us to put our cars, our tow trucks, and our tractor trailers to good

Get Going

use, and do what God has designed us to do so that we can be part of the bigger picture. God has a plan for each of us and all of our plans put together are part of a bigger picture. One day we will be able to see and understand the roles we have in God's overall plan. We will then realize how important it is for us to serve God in the way He wants.

So remember, a healthy running, restored car is of no use if it just sits in the garage. I can't imagine putting the time and effort into restoring my 1973 Corvette, just to have it sit in the garage. It was built to drive. So that's what I'm going to do. I'm going to put the top down and go cruising down the path that God takes me, being careful to avoid getting into accidents. I'm going to be an active part of God's bigger picture.

It's your turn now. I believe that you know that God is the right choice, and you have faith that God will lead, guide, and direct you. Now it is up to you to put your car in gear and get into the action. So what are you waiting for?

Driver Check List: *Go into the world - Matthew 28:19-20*

- *If you haven't started implementing the chapters of this book into your life, go back and start today!*
- *Don't wait until tomorrow, now is the time to start being active.*
- *Change your life, and say "Yes" to God!*

Chapter 9: Exploring on Your Own

In the following section I have included some analogies for you to explore on your own. I encourage you to take some time to think about how you can better understand your relationship with God by thinking in terms of a car. Perhaps there are some other analogies that you come up with on your own. I encourage you to write them down so that you can come back and revisit them later. You can also share your ideas with others online at www.carsandchristianity.com.

Keep your eyes on the road and not the rearview mirror:
(Isaiah 43:18-19, Philippians 3:13-14)

_____
_____
_____
_____
_____
_____
_____
_____
_____
_____
_____
_____
_____
_____
_____
_____
_____

For online discussion and interaction visit:
www.carsandchristianity.com

Exploring on Your Own

Relying on a tow truck or road side assistance when you find yourself getting stuck: (1 Thessalonians 5:11, James 5:13-16)

_____
_____
_____
_____
_____
_____
_____
_____
_____
_____
_____
_____
_____

Obey the speed limit: (Psalm 46:10, Proverbs 19:2)

_____
_____
_____
_____
_____
_____
_____
_____
_____
_____
_____
_____
_____

For online discussion and interaction visit:
www.carsandchristianity.com

For online discussion and interaction visit:
www.carsandchristianity.com

CARS
AND
CHRISTIANITY